OUR FATHER

OUR FATHER

A STUDY OF THE
LORD'S PRAYER

BY

ANTHONY C. DEANE, M.A.

VICAR OF ALL SAINTS, ENNISMORE GARDENS
AND HON. CANON OF WORCESTER CATHEDRAL

HODDER AND STOUGHTON
LIMITED   LONDON

MADE AND PRINTED IN GREAT BRITAIN
BY JARROLD AND SONS LTD. NORWICH

General Preface ❧ ❧ ❧ ❧

*T*HE Christian life is a many-sided thing, as many-sided as life itself, since all life is meant to be Christian. It includes belief and conduct; experience and hope; prayer and service; church and home and daily task; the joy of a divine revelation, and the upward climb of the loftiest ethic the world has ever known. And according to the history and environment of each soul who tries to live the life are the facets which Christianity reveals and the problems it brings to light. These little books are intended to treat various aspects of this many-sided theme in a brief and interesting way, in a form pleasant to handle and attractive not least to younger readers.

7

Contents ✐ ✐ ✐ ✐ ✐

Chapter I

INTRODUCTION

I. Introduction ◦ ◦ ◦

I

NO other form of words has a hold upon mankind like the few brief sentences of the Lord's Prayer. Not a day has passed without their use since that far time when Jesus taught them to His disciples. These were the first words we learnt by heart as little children, so that they are fragrant with memories of love and innocency. And they are the last to be forgotten by men who have lost all else of religion. They are recited by every Christian Church, in every service, from baptism to burial. They are at the heart of private devotion. People who differ on a hundred points of doctrine are linked by their common use of the Lord's Prayer. If much seems uncertain when we try, from our so different points of view, to interpret the mind of the Master, at least we know beyond doubt that we do His will when we pray "Our Father . . ."

Yet because it is so familiar we have the more need to guard against using the Prayer in mechanic fashion, or with only a dim sense of its meaning. Many books have been written to expound it, but their chief aim, for the most part, is to apply the Prayer's teaching to contemporary problems of social life and conduct. Exposition of that kind has been done in our own time with skill and thoroughness, so that there seems no present need to repeat it. But there is need, I think, for renewed study of another kind, which strictly should come first of all—a study less of the supposed implications of the Prayer than of the Prayer itself, a close scrutiny of its wording. For if we are to use the Prayer rightly, we must try to know the exact significance of its petitions. If we would relate its teaching with ethical and social problems, at the start we must make ourselves sure what

14

hat teaching is. We must neither rob
he sentences of their full import,
1or read into them an imagined mean-
ng.

Of this the risk is greater, perhaps,
than might be supposed. A very large
proportion of those who use the Lord's
Prayer have but a general sense of its
meaning, and quite misunderstand some
of its phrases. This happens partly because they have never examined the
sentences in detail, being content to
take them, as it were, on trust ; and
partly because often they retain through
later years some inaccurate interpretation
given in their schooldays. An immense
amount of fresh light has been thrown
upon the language of the New Testament
within the past few decades, and a very
real need of our time is that this knowledge
should be popularized, should be trans-
ferred from technical treatises and jour-
nals so as to become the ordinary heritage
of ordinary folk. As things are now,
the new Testament of scholars is a quite

different book from the New Testament of the average educated Englishman.

This book, then, is to be written with the single aim of studying the Lord's Prayer, not in its remoter applications, but in its direct and immediate significance. This is to be done by scrutinizing the actual wording of the Prayer, so that we may range ourselves beside the disciples to whom first it was given. Often, too, the significance of a phrase, the intent of its teaching, becomes clearer when we set beside it other words spoken by the Master on the same theme. All this should be no arid, intellectual study ; rather it should help us to use the Prayer with a devotion heightened by understanding. If a word of personal witness be allowed, I would say that for me the beauty and the richness and practical helpfulness of the Paternoster were increased by detailed study of it to a degree I had never expected. And I shall be content indeed if this book can help others to a like experience.

Introduction

II

We will begin with a few preliminary points. The English form of the Prayer, which we all have by heart—that containing the word "trespasses"—comes not from the Authorized or Revised Versions of the Bible, but from the Book of Common Prayer, which in turn derived it from earlier English service-books. For the most part, however, it agrees with the later (1611) rendering of the Prayer in St. Matthew given by the Authorized Version. Beyond doubt, the doxology at the close ("for Thine is the Kingdom," etc.) was not of the Prayer as our Lord taught it, for it is missing from the best MSS. of St. Matthew. When the Paternoster came early to be used in public worship, these words were added to it, as a very appropriate act of praise. Afterwards some scribe, transcribing the First Gospel and knowing the Prayer in its liturgical form, would assume these words to have been left out in error from the text he copied. In his own, therefore, he would append the doxology, and afterwards other scribes would copy his work without question. Thus the sentences which begin "For Thine is the Kingdom" came to be given a place in many texts of the first Gospel. The Prayer-book adopts them when the Lord's Prayer is used in a service of praise, and omits them at other times. We may well follow this example in private use, yet remembering that the words are a supplement to the Lord's Prayer, and not a part of it as taught by Christ.

But more important than this detail is a question which may have perplexed the reader, and indeed has been a theme of debate among experts. There are two versions of the Paternoster—one in the First Gospel, the other in the Third. They are notably different, both in wording and setting. According to St. Matthew, the Lord's Prayer was spoken as part of the Sermon on the Mount, and followed some general teaching on the right method of praying. According to St. Luke, it was given at a quite other time, in answer to a request from a disciple. We will compare the two narratives and forms of the Prayer, quoting the Revised Version, which here is far more accurate than the Authorized :

St. Matthew vi, 9–13

After this manner therefore pray ye :
    Our Father which art in heaven,
    Hallowed be thy name.
    Thy kingdom come.
    Thy will be done, as in heaven, so on
      earth.
    Give us this day our daily bread.
    And forgive us our debts, as we also have
      forgiven our debtors.
    And bring us not into temptation, but
      deliver us from evil.

St. Luke xi, 1–4

And it came to pass, as he was praying in a certain place, that when he ceased, one of his disciples said unto him, Lord, teach us to pray, even as John also taught his disciples   And he said unto them, When ye pray, say,

> Father,
> Hallowed be thy name.
> Thy kingdom come.
> Give us day by day our daily bread.
> And forgive us our sins ; for we ourselves
>   also forgive every one that is indebted
>   to us.
> And bring us not into temptation.

The seeming discrepancies are plain. Which Gospel, then, it has been asked, records rightly the occasion of the Prayer ? Which preserves the true wording ? Did the Third Gospel abbreviate the Prayer, or the First expand it ?

Concerning the first of these questions, we may feel sure that St. Luke's narrative is true to fact, and that the Prayer was spoken, as he describes, when a disciple had begged " Lord, teach us to pray." It is incredible that St. Luke invented this story. It is not incredible, on the other hand, that the writer of the

Introduction

First Gospel, setting down in the Sermon on the Mount our Lord's directions about praying, should insert immediately after them the Prayer which the Lord Himself taught. If, then, the Prayer were spoken but once by the Master, we may believe the occasion to be described rightly by St. Luke.

Of greater importance is the other question. Is the Prayer as spoken by our Lord represented more faithfully by the Matthæan version or the Lucan? The divergences between them are even greater than our English translations make plain. In Greek, I find that there are fifty-seven words in St. Matthew's version. Only twenty-five of these are used identically by St. Luke. Twenty-two words are omitted entirely by him. The remaining ten are changed to different forms.

A close study of the problem thought to arise from these facts would compel the examination of technical details outside the scope of this book. Let it suffice to state results. The judgment of scholars has confirmed the choice made by the Church when it took the form given in St. Matthew's Gospel for daily use. The text of the Lord's Prayer as we all have learnt and say it is, we have full right to believe, in accordance with words spoken by Jesus Christ. It has been thought by many that the two evangelists must have had before them the same Greek version of the Prayer, as both reproduce one word which has been found nowhere else in Greek, either of the New Testament or elsewhere. If so, we may believe more easily that St. Luke shortened the Prayer than that St. Matthew lengthened it. Some of St. Luke's changes can be explained ; once or twice, for instance, he seems, without making any substantial change of sense, to replace a word by another he himself liked and used often in his writings. As for his omissions, these too have been explained. Thus it has been supposed that he held the petition " Thy Kingdom come " to imply and include " Thy will be done," so that the meaning was complete without these latter words. On the whole, then, scholars find it not difficult to account for the alterations they suppose St. Luke to have made.

On the other hand, they believe the longer form of St. Matthew to be the more accurate. The Prayer was meant to be committed to memory, and, as an aid to this, the Rabbis (whose methods our Lord adopted) were wont to clothe such teaching in a symmetrical form. And the Lord's Prayer of the Matthæan version is strictly symmetrical. After the opening words of address there are six petitions : three for God's glory, three for our needs. Of the first three, the dominant word is " Thy "—" Thy name," " Thy Kingdom," " Thy will." Of the second three, the dominant word is " us " : " Give us," " Forgive us," " bring us." (As we shall see later, " but deliver us " is not a separate petition.) To sum up, then : if the

Prayer were delivered but once, St. Luke best describes the occasion, St. Matthew best gives us the wording of the Prayer; and it is St. Matthew's version which we have learnt to use.

III

Yet was the Prayer taught but once? Until lately scholars have been quite curiously apt to take this for granted. None the less, it is an assumption which does violence both to human nature and to all we know of educational methods in our Lord's time. Through the years of His ministry He came before mankind as a Rabbi. Thus He was known and thus addressed, alike by His disciples, by the multitude, by His enemies. He taught on themes which none but accredited Rabbis might touch. He sat to teach—the recognized posture of a Rabbi. And the method of a Rabbi was to select from his general instruction

24

certain things which seemed of a chief importance, and to say these many times to his disciples, until they had them by heart, or at least were sure of their meaning. A teacher who had framed prayers for his disciples (as many Rabbis did, and as the Baptist had done for his followers) would repeat them many times. It is for commentators who assume our Lord to have departed from this practice to show any evidence for their view. And, in fact, there is none.

Again, quite apart from the Rabbinical methods Jesus employed, is it in the least likely that He would speak His Prayer on one occasion only ? St. Luke describes a moment when " a disciple "— unnamed, and presumably not of the Twelve—asked the Master for a model prayer. May we not feel sure that other disciples at other times would make the same request ? And, when once our Lord had framed the Prayer, would He not, of His own accord, repeat it to different groups of people, and in the different places He visited ? It seems likely enough that, while its essence would be always the same, its details of wording might be varied, perhaps the better to suit the audience before Him at the moment. We know now—until lately it was quite unsuspected—that the Jews were bilingual, speaking Greek as well as Aramaic. In Aramaic, no doubt, the most of our Lord's converse was held, but it is possible—perhaps even probable—that, at one time or another, He spoke the Prayer in Greek. Thus again there would be small variations of detail in the wording.

In fact, the scholastic dilemma which sets us to choose between the two settings and versions of the Paternoster has, I believe, no real existence. No doubt the authorities are right who tell us to credit the story of St. Luke. No doubt they are right when they bid us accept the wording of the Prayer as given by St. Matthew. Only it does not follow that the setting ascribed to the Prayer by St. Matthew is wrong, or that the version of the Prayer recorded by St. Luke was never spoken. Far more probably, I think, both Evangelists are accurate, and bring us two of the various forms and two of the many times in which the Lord's Prayer was delivered.

Let us return for a moment to St. Luke's narrative. A disciple came and said, " Lord, teach us to pray." Perhaps Jesus long had wished to do that. But, as with His works of healing, He seems ever to have been constrained by a law which forbade Him to give until man had asked for the gift, had shown his sense of need. No sooner had the disciple said, " Teach us to pray," than the Prayer was bestowed. There was no delay during which it was shaped into studied form. Rather, that which was spoken, and recorded by St. Luke, proved, in effect, an extemporized first draft. Thus its unsymmetrical and comparatively brief form is to be understood. Later, our Lord would develop this first draft.

He would expand the original wording. He would perfect the form, dividing the whole into two sections of three petitions apiece, thereby making it the more easy to remember. Afterwards He might include this perfected form in His Sermon on the Mount, according to St. Matthew's record. Anyhow, He would use it in His subsequent teaching. The complete and symmetrical form would be that which His followers would learn by heart and transmit to the Church. St. Luke's version would be the first extempore sketch of it, given without premeditation in the circumstances he describes. Thus the two accounts of the two Evangelists become not contradictory, but complementary.

IV

There is one other point of seeming discrepancy, and again the true explanation may be of the same kind. St.

Matthew's words are, " After this manner pray ye " ; St. Luke's, " When ye pray, say "—so that, according to the former, this Prayer is to be taken as a model for prayers of our own ; according to the latter, it is a prayer actually to be recited as it stands. But are not both accounts of it true ? We may accept it, surely, both as one the wording of which is to be taken on our own lips, and one the spirit of which is to serve as a pattern when we pray, " after this fashion." Long usage of the Prayer shows us continually new stores of richness in its meaning. And the prayers we make for ourselves accord with the mind of God in proportion as their spirit and wide range and unselfishness reproduce the spirit of that pattern prayer which Jesus gave.

Thus we will turn to examine closely the wording of that Prayer, both in order that thereby we may come nearer to a right understanding of its significance, and also because to know the Lord's Prayer is to know how to pray.

Our Father

That which we attempt need be no frigidly academic study, but rather an effort to come and learn of Christ, as the people of Galilee came, because we want to know how to pray better, and therefore to understand better the greatest Prayer of all.

CHAPTER II

THE HALLOWING OF THE NAME

II. The Hallowing of the Name ↝

I

WHEN we consider the Prayer as a whole, we shall be impressed anew by its exquisite beauty of structure. Of this many people have never taken note. Yet it is of far more than a merely literary interest. It confirms, I think, the view that the Prayer in its complete form—the Matthæan form we all use—could not have been extemporized at a disciple's request, as was, apparently, that first sketch of the Prayer which St. Luke describes. Again, the precise balance of symmetry of form seems to prove that here we have what we may term the considered work of Christ. The Prayer has for me a value even greater than before when I feel that our Lord Himself thus clearly showed the importance He attached to it, working upon and revising it until this concentrated expression of His teaching, this noblest of all prayers, had become clothed in a form of wonderful beauty.

Let us look at that rather more closely before studying the individual phrases. We have seen already that the whole is made up of seven sentences—first, the words of address, and then two groups of three petitions each : the first three for God's glory, the second three for human needs. And it is not merely fanciful to remember that for those to whom our Lord spoke seven and three were " sacred " numbers, fraught with mystic meaning. Next, we may observe how each sentence of a group matches the corresponding sentence in the other group. As Dr. Plummer has pointed out, the first petition is addressed to God as our Father, the second as our King, the third as our Master. And so in the second triplet it is to our Father that we look for sustenance, to our King for pardon, to our Master for guardianship.

And again, " If we take the six petitions consecutively, we shall find that they begin with the glories of heaven, pass on to life on earth, and end with the powers of hell." There are further details of symmetry and parallelism which will become clear to all who will be at the pains to examine the structure with care. And, apart from their intrinsic beauty, they show us beyond doubt that the Lord's Prayer is not, so to speak, a casual assemblage of petitions for His disciples' use, but an organic whole, thought out and contrived with transcendent skill and care. We may be sure that it did not cost our Lord nothing to achieve this work, to weld the unsymmetric sentences of the earlier form into this masterpiece. And the Prayer must have the greater value and significance to ourselves because, thus clearly, it meant so much to Him Who made it.

As we approach the three petitions which compose the first part, there is one other detail of arrangement to be noticed at the outset. It is not clearly to be discerned in our versions, yet it seems to have a real importance. We may justly feel certain, I believe, that the words " as in heaven, so on earth " (such is their order in the Greek phrase) qualify each of the three petitions making up the first part of the Prayer. They do not refer, that is, to the doing of the will alone, but equally to the hallowing of the Name and the coming of the Kingdom. Thus this first part of the Prayer is :

> Our Father in heaven !
> As in heaven, so on earth,
>   Thy Name be hallowed,
>   Thy Kingdom come,
>   Thy will be done.

Does not that link in a very beautiful way the three petitions, showing one great thought that runs through each ? We do not merely ask, in a general and abstract way, for the hallowing of the

Name, the coming of the Kingdom, and then, more precisely, for the doing of the will on earth as in heaven. Rather, the whole paragraph glows, from start to finish, with the same magnificent idealism. This springs, so to speak, from the opening words of address. We lift our hearts to God as our Father in heaven, and the use of that term leads us to ask that, as in heaven, so here on earth by us, He may be reverenced, honoured, and obeyed.

Is it not true that for many of us there will be new cogency and force in the first part of the Lord's Prayer when we keep this sense in our minds ?

II

Now let us look closely at the wording and its significance.

As St. Luke records the Prayer, the opening address consists of the single word " Father." In the complete Matthæan version, we have, translating literally, " Our Father, the (Father) in the heavens." It were needless to insist upon the import of the pronoun ; that is as clear as it is beautiful. It implies the doctrine of Christian brotherhood. The man who in uttermost solitude uses the Lord's Prayer must perforce pray not only for himself but for all his brethren. The man who in dejection might doubt if his weak prayers were worthy to be heard is made sure that with his own are linked the prayers of all within the brotherhood of Christ. The Creed, even when recited by a multitude, must be separate and individual; " I believe," since none may do another's believing for him ; the Prayer, even when said in stark isolation, must be collective and social, " Our Father . . . Give us . . ." since love and unselfishness are at the very heart of all true prayer.

It will be noticed that the Greek word at the close of the opening phrase is " heavens," not " heaven." Not much stress need be laid on this, as the

plural and singular seem to be used often
with no distinction of meaning. But we
may remember the Jewish belief, echoed
by St. Paul, in a series of " heavens," so
that the grammarians may be right who
term this a " plural of majesty "—the
thought being that the Father pervades
and rules all the heavens. Again, though,
the phrase may be taken—and more
rightly, I think—as merely the equivalent
of an adjective. " Father in heaven "
and " heavenly Father " seem to be used
indifferently throughout the Gospels.
And the thought linked thereto in the
teaching of Christ seems to be one not
of locality but quality. His eager desire
was to show not *where* God is, but *what*
God is. He gave no special revelation
about the setting of life in its next stage,
being content to reproduce, as in the
Dives and Lazarus parable, ideas current
among His audience. " Your heavenly
Father " in His speech meant not chiefly
a Father Who " dwells in Heaven," but
a Father Who is perfect. " Heavenly,"

in His mind stands, then, for " perfection," and human life on " earth " for imperfection.

Many passages to illustrate this will occur to the reader, as, for instance, " If ye then, being evil, know how to give good gifts to your children, how much more shall your heavenly Father . . ." Of all, however, the most significant is the sentence ending the Sermon on the Mount : " Be ye therefore perfect, even as your Father which is in heaven is perfect." That command accords completely with the opening sentence of the Paternoster. It propounds the ideal at which, though we cannot achieve it, we are to try to aim. With nothing less are we to be satisfied. And so, saying the words of address in the Prayer, the thought they are meant to bring is not the lifting of our voice to One far withdrawn in illimitable heights, but rather the thought that we turn to Him Who is Perfect, and make His perfection the measure of our aspirations. " O Perfect

Father, perfectly even here on earth, may Thy Name be hallowed, Thy Kingdom come, Thy will be done ! " That sets the key, the highest possible key, for the whole.

III

" Our Father," the Prayer begins. In Greek " Father " is the first word of the first sentence. We might wish it could have the same place in the English version, for there is no one word more characteristic of the Prayer's Maker, no word the use of which distinguishes more clearly His teaching from that of all the prophets and wise men before Him. It occurs but seven times in all the Old Testament, but there can have been scarce a day when Jesus did not use it. During the centuries separating Old Testament from New there was very much development of religious thought ; the belief in personal immortality, the idea of a Divine Kingdom to come, were

strengthened vastly within those four
and a half centuries, and so prepared
the way for the teaching of Christ. But
the concept of God's Fatherhood was
still quite indistinct ; so far as it took
shape, it viewed God's paternal relationship as existing not between Himself
and individual souls, but merely between
Himself and the Jewish nation as a community, and its sense did not go beyond
an attempt to blend in one word
the thoughts of God as Creator and
Ruler.

Thus we have need to remember how
startling and how novel was that doctrine
of the Fatherhood which Jesus bestowed
upon the world. It was His concrete
manner of insisting that God is love.
The relationship He described was not
merely that between Creator and created,
but that pictured once for all in the
parable of the Prodigal Son. There is,
Jesus insisted, a spiritual kinship between
God and man ; we are His children, and
(as St. Paul says) " because we are sons,

42

we cry, Abba, Father." In a brief study of the Lord's Prayer it would be out of place to enter on a long discussion of all that Christ's teaching of the Fatherhood implies. Yet it is a needful, and a happy, thing for us to have in mind, that when we begin His Prayer we are encouraged by our Lord to address ourselves to God not as a great invisible power, not as a despot, not even merely as our Creator, but as " our Father," as perfect Love, to Whom, with the simple trustfulness and frankness of little children, we are to tell our wants.

IV

Yet this view of God may be, indeed sometimes has been, so over-emphasized, so perverted out of all due proportion, as to become misleading and dangerous. Then the idea of the Fatherhood is degraded, as someone has said, to a kind of magnified Eli, and the thought of God's illimitable righteousness and majesty is sentimentalized away. The Lord's Prayer is phrased as if Jesus were mindful of this danger. The opening word brings us to the Father, fills us with this new revelation of His tender love for each of His children. Yet our Lord, while giving this, would not weaken that tremendous sense of awe in approaching Him which had possessed the Jews through long generations. Because God was henceforth to be known as the Father, more, and not less than before, must the thought of Him fill us with humblest reverence. So we see again the exquisite poise and balance in the teaching of Jesus, shown by the structure of His Prayer. Having been taught to invoke God as " Our Father," immediately the first petition that follows is that we may honour Him profoundly on earth, even as the angels do in heaven. First " Our Father," and then immediately, " Hallowed be Thy Name."

The meaning of this petition would be evident to all whom Jesus taught, for it was an accustomed beginning to Jewish prayers. But its force is less generally understood by people of our own time, who often do not realize for what "Name" stood, in Jewish usage. And indeed its precise force is less easy to set down in English words. But, approximately, "God's Name" meant God as He disclosed Himself to man. The Name is not an impersonal revelation about God, but God as He has vouchsafed to show Himself. And so the prayer is that He may be worshipped and held in profoundest awe, that the Truth He has revealed of Himself may be held most sacred, that most humbly we on earth may do Him homage, even as do the triumphant hosts of heaven. As we use these words, we ourselves worship; we pray that we may ever do so rightly; and we ask that everywhere God's revelation of Himself may be received and reverenced. We echo the cry of *Magnificat*, " and holy is His Name," and our prayer is akin to that which the Fourth

Gospel attributes to our Lord Himself:
" Father, glorify Thy Name."

So the meaning of the first petition
becomes clear, and the need that we
should make it is greater than it was for
the disciples who first heard the Prayer.
In our age the danger is more consider-
able of losing that sense of awe with
which we should approach God. The
sentence has a special import for us in
our study of the Bible and in our theo-
logical discussions. It is good for us to
examine God's revelation, to ponder
the union of human and divine in the
Person and words of our Lord, to bring
all modern knowledge—which is, indeed,
a part of God's revelation—to aid the
conclusions at which we arrive. Yet
assuredly we shall miss our way unless we
undertake such studies in the right spirit,
losing nothing of the infinite awe with
which the saints of old touched holy
things.

In ordinary life and speech, again, we
need to pray for a deeper sense of rever-

ence. God reveals Himself in many ways
—through the Christ Who " declared
His Name," through nature, through
experience. We need to treat all this
revelation as deeply sacred, and be
resolved that it shall not be disparaged
through us for those who come after.
Through our example, we ask, through
our lives, through our spirit of lowly
awe, Hallowed be Thy Name!

Chapter III

THE KINGDOM

III. *The Kingdom* ❧   ❧   ❧

I

AN early sentence of the earliest
Evangelist states that "Jesus came
preaching the Gospel of the Kingdom
of God." The phrase might be
used to epitomize almost all His public
ministry. The Kingdom was ever His
dominant theme. By deed and by example, no less than by word, He toiled
to expound it. We can scarce turn a
page of the Gospels without finding
some reference to "the Kingdom of
God"—or its equivalent, in St. Matthew,
"the Kingdom of Heaven." It is the
central *motif* of our Lord's teaching.
The Kingdom is to be sought before all
else. No sacrifice is too great which
may make entrance to it less difficult.
The laws and conditions of finding place
within it are laid down, and even to be

not far from it is high encouragement.
With indefatigable labour the Master
tries to make plain this doctrine of the
Kingdom. "Unto what shall we liken
it?" He asks, and replies with a suc-
cession of swift and vivid pictures which
may help His hearers to understand.
It is like a grain of mustard-seed, like
leaven, like a net, like a man sowing, like
a pearl of great price, like a treasure in
comparison with which all others are
nothing worth.

Because the Kingdom has a place so
large in the doctrine of Jesus it has been
studied eagerly in each age of the Church,
and interpreted from many different
points of view. Perhaps the chief con-
tribution of our own time towards understanding it rightly has been to discern
its comprehensiveness. Most of the past
interpreters were right when they claimed
that their understanding of the doctrine
accorded with words spoken by Christ,
but were wrong in supposing this one line
of interpretation to be sufficient, and all

others to be needless or mistaken. It was a very wide, as well as a very deep, idea that our Lord set before mankind when He preached the Gospel of the Kingdom. Plainly, anything like a full study of the teaching about the Kingdom of God could not be attempted here. It has formed the theme of many volumes, and will form the theme, doubtless, of many more. On the other hand, we are bound to arrive, if we can, at the central idea of the phrase as our Lord employed it, for we cannot use the Lord's Prayer well until we know what it is we ask when we pray " Thy Kingdom come." We must wish to find not so much a meaning for the words which satisfies modern conceptions as the meaning they had for our Lord, and the reason why He bade His disciples use them in the supreme Prayer.

II

Through centuries the Jews had looked
for the coming of a Kingdom of God.
This belief might seem to make easier
the task of Christ, since to speak of the
Kingdom was to use a word familiar
already, and to name that which the
coming Messiah was expected to establish.
Yet it was a hindrance too, because,
while " the Kingdom of God " was an
accustomed phrase, the meaning in which
our Lord used it was altogether new.
Thus He had to explain, by much exposition and many illustrative parables,
that His idea of the Kingdom was remote
from many that His hearers had known.
The meaning He gave it was as strange
as the phrase itself was familiar. It had
been the theme of Apocalyptic through
about two centuries before Christ came,
and these writings had made the people
look forward to a sudden manisfestation
of Divine power. The coming of the

Kingdom meant partly the restitution of the Jewish people and the overthrow of alien rule. But it had a spiritual side also—the vindication of righteousness and the destruction of those who had rejected God. Some supposed that the Kingdom would be established in this world, others in the next. All anticipated that it would be heralded by a sudden and catastrophic manifestation of the Divine sovereignty. A very large literature fostered this belief, and it served to console Israel through years of subjugation to Roman rule. When they heard John the Baptist, the people believed that the day of freedom and the advent of the national leader were at hand.

Jesus spoke, then, to people steeped in this belief—people looking anxiously for the coming of the Kingdom of God. But they expected it to be local, and national, and sudden ; Jesus meant it to be worldwide, and spiritual, and of slow growth. In His view it was to be not outward but inward ; to take effect not through a reformed government but through a transformed heart. It was to bring all human life into the realm of God. Its basis was to be character, and all the Sermon on the Mount was a description of the kind of character for which there can be place within the Kingdom, and of the laws, the new kind of " righteousness," by which such a character will be controlled. Moreover, it was to be a kingdom having Christ Himself for its Founder and its King.

So much seems clear. Yet there remain questions to be asked concerning Christ's view of the Kingdom of God. Did it seem to Him a present reality or a future ideal ? Was it to be an invisible union linking together His followers, or was it to possess a definite and visible organization ? If so, was it but another name for the Church ? Again, ought its scope to be limited to the spiritual life, or should it have relations with the social and political systems of each age ?

We may answer, I think, that the

Kingdom of God as our Lord saw it was both present and future. On the one hand, He spoke of it as having come already and being in the midst of the disciples ; on the other, He referred to those who should see its coming with power in a far future. Here His teaching was sometimes in close likeness to that of Apocalyptic. But He insisted also that the Kingdom was present already, and would grow like a grain of mustard seed. Thus it was both a gift to be received and an ideal to be achieved. Again, the Kingdom was not one with the Church, though the business of the Church must be to help forward its growth and to guard what has been gained already for the Kingdom. To the remaining question, perhaps our first reply must be that the supposed boundary line between, on the one hand, the " spiritual," and, the other, the political and social aspects of human life, does not properly exist, and that many of our worst blunders have their root in this false distinction. Yet dealing with the question as it stands, we may affirm that our Lord left us in no doubt concerning the practical effect of His Kingdom upon the life of the world. It would transform that life, but it would bring to pass the changes very slowly, and working from within. There would be no sudden and dramatic upheaval, such as the Jews had expected. There would be no revolution in the forms of government or in the social fabric. The Kingdom would begin by changing not institutions but men. Slowly, like leaven, its influence would spread, until the whole mass of human life was altered by its power. The method was to be not of changed institutions in the hope of bringing to pass a better life, but of a changed life which in time would create better institutions. The Kingdom of God " within you " must be the source of the Kingdom without.

58

III

All this is, of course, but a summary of truths with which by this time most of us are well acquainted. They have been put before us, with a large measure of agreement, by various writers who have set themselves to study our Lord's conception of " the Kingdom of God." They are conclusions not likely to be overthrown, and they have rightly displaced mistaken theories about the Kingdom—especially those which identified it exclusively with the Church, and those which, in effect, postponed the advent of the Kingdom to " the end of the world." Valuable, however, as they are, and true so far as they go, I doubt if, by themselves, they are quite adequate. They lay down a very beautiful and logical system of development. They reconcile various sayings of our Lord which hitherto had seemed discrepant. But may they not be just a little too lucid, definite, and

concrete ? When we want to know for
what the Kingdom of God stood in the
mind of Jesus, it is natural that we should
concentrate our attention upon those
sayings of His in which He speaks of it
directly. And this is, in the main, what
scholars have done, and done most admir-
ably, in recent years. Yet I dare to
think that a wider view is needed, and
that we learn of the significance which
" the Kingdom " held for our Lord not
more from special passages of His teaching
than from the whole tenor of His life,
His whole outlook on the relations between God and man. When we try to
take such a view we place ourselves neces-
sarily farther from framing precise and
convenient definitions, but nearer, may-
be, to understanding the mind of Christ.

For surely the teaching of the Kingdom
was not meant merely to propound one
special scheme of human development,
or one special method of divine guidance.
Rather, it was an attempt to set forth a
vast idea embracing all existence, in this

stage of life and beyond, " as in heaven, so on earth." The idea in its fullness transcends all human speech, and our Lord Himself could not find any one form of words or illustration to describe it adequately. He must be content if by reiterated teaching, by clothing now this, now another aspect of it in a parable, He might at length make partly clear to His disciples what was so luminously evident to Himself.

Life, as He saw it, was not a transient physical condition—which was, relatively, of small importance. To live was to be in right relation with God, to be permeated with the sense of His all-pervading nearness and holiness and love and power. Our Lord Himself was ever thrilled through and through with this consciousness of the Father, to do Whose will, therefore, must be the passion and glory of all true life. Let any man truly realize God, and he must love Him and his fellow-men ; this sense of God must become his overmastering and eager enthusiasm, dominating every act and thought. Then, from sheer love, God would be his King, and so, acknowledging and serving Him in joy, a man would pass from death into life, would gain place in the Kingdom of God. With him would be linked others afire with the same enthusiasm for God, and so the Kingdom would become a visible society in this world, so its influence would spread. If only men would overcome the sin or blindness which shuts their eyes to the joy of serving God ! If only they would simplify existence and gain freedom from care by making the doing of His will their one law ! What happiness would be theirs, and how the world would be transformed ! Already there were a few who had entered on this life, in whom something like a true consciousness of God's immanent power and love was beginning to dawn ; through these, and through His own work, the Kingdom was already here. " The Kingdom of God is among you ! " Yet how few were within its sway, how many without! Therefore let the disciple pray " Thy Kingdom come." To open the gateway of the soul that the glory of God might pour through it, to let the inward rush of power dominate the life until every thought and act became its outcome, to merge human will joyously in the divine will until a single motive co-ordinated all existence—that, it seems, was the life which Jesus Himself lived, such the life He described to others under the figure of entering the Kingdom of God.

IV

At least such an explanation brings us nearer, I believe, to the real meaning of the phrase as our Lord used it than the more precise and literal interpretations of the accustomed type. The Kingdom, then, is not a social organization, or an institution, or an event to come. Rather, it is an attempt to describe figuratively the one true mode of life, life begun here with a physical setting, but indestructible by what we name death. And to make that view understood more easily our Lord set it forth under the figure of the Kingdom, because for the advent of a Kingdom of God the people were looking. Yet if we find it hard to realize our Lord's standpoint, to see life as He saw it, can we wonder that His ideal baffled most of those to whom He spoke ? God was for them a being awful and remote. Righteousness was a technical virtue, which began and ended with a mechanical observance of the Rabbinic code. The whole teaching of Jesus was bewildering novel. " What is this ? A new doctrine ! " they cried in amazement. Only those who were ready to trust and to try, to experiment by leading the kind of life which the Master prescribed, found that it made all things clear, that the due love of God and neighbour were its logical outcome. Thereafter they might fail often to realize the ideal. But no longer could they doubt what the true ideal was. To lead a life hid with Christ in God was to enter the Kingdom. To strive that all men might share this overmastering consciousness of God was to pray " Thy Kingdom come "—to ask and to work that God's sovereignty might be complete everywhere, in earth as in heaven.

So we return to this sentence of the Paternoster. What is it that most people have in mind when they say, " Thy Kingdom come " ? With a few, retaining unconsciously the old Apocalyptic idea, it is a prayer for the speedy return of Christ as King, and the end of the world. Others take the sentence as asking only that their inner hearts may obey Christ and conquer the rival powers of evil. Yet others, influenced by the tradition which St. Augustine did much to popularize, take the Kingdom to be but another name for the Church, and discern in this sentence merely a prayer for the Church's progress. But, as we have seen, none of these interpretations is satisfying or adequate. Our Lord's words about the end of the world are coloured so largely by, and take so much of their imagery from, the Apocalyptic writings that it seems rash to interpret them with a crude literalism. And, unmistakably, " Thy Kingdom come " was meant to be a prayer for the world's trend, not for the world's end. With reiterated emphasis He made it clear that the Kingdom was to be set up in this world—was, indeed, already here when He spoke, even though its full completion must be hereafter. Of the second interpretation we need say no more than that this petition must not be made virtually identical with that which stands later in the Prayer, " Lead us not into temptation, but deliver us from evil." And lastly, while to pray for the work of the Church must obviously be right, and while the growth of the Church may be a witness to the growth of the Kingdom, nevertheless the Kingdom is distinct from, and wider than, the Church.

We must not narrow the spirit of the Prayer.

V

And is not the wider meaning—in a sense, more simple, yet more profound—that also which satisfies best, and gives the words their richest meaning? In the soul of Jesus, we may say with all reverence, the reign of God was supreme. He longed, and bade us pray, that this glorious consciousness of, and obedience to, God's reign should be shared by all human beings. That, surely, is what we ask when we pray "Thy Kingdom come."

We ask it first for the glory of God, because it is His due. The pronoun of these sentences is emphatic in the original "as in heaven, so on earth, Thine be the Name hallowed, Thine be the Kingdom to come, Thine the will to be done." The great reason of these three petitions is the advancement of God's glory; petitions for our own needs follow in the second part of the Prayer. Yet, mindful that we ask it primarily for God's sake, we may make the request for ourselves also, because there can be no happiness like that which comes from having God enthroned in our souls. And we ask it for others also, both that God's purpose may be completed, and that the great community of those whose lives are dominated by the consciousness of God may increase, as Jesus desired.

For, indeed, this magnificent petition includes all prayers for our organized social life, and, in a sense, makes them superfluous. We pray for the growth of the Church, for a spirit of concord among Christians, for peace among nations, for an ending of rancour and strife between classes, for social righteousness—we can multiply such intercessions almost endlessly, and the need of them is real. But could we bring about the perfect fulfilment (" as in heaven, so on earth ") of this one thing, " Thy Kingdom come," all else for which we pray would follow.

The Kingdom

When once the reign of God pervaded the hearts of men, when once His realm was everything to them, as it was to our Lord, what social problem or bitterness would not be in sight of its end ? All these things would " be added " to us, if first, by prayer and deed, we sought the Kingdom of God, and set ourselves to bring nearer that which, in very truth, we ask for when we pray " Thy Kingdom come ! "

Chapter IV

THE DOING OF THE WILL

IV. The Doing of the Will ❧ ❧

I

ALREADY we have seen the Paternoster to be no string of unrelated petitions, brought together without premeditated design, but a symmetrical structure, framed with exquisite skill. And at this point let us pause for a moment to observe the manner in which in this first part of the Prayer each sentence leads logically to the next. We begin by praying that God's revelation of Himself may be held in perfect awe and reverence. What can stir that awe and reverence in the hearts of men ? That they should live in a radiant sense of God, in a consciousness of His all-pervading realm and its claims ; in other words, that they should be within His Kingdom. In order, therefore, that His name may be hallowed rightly, we ask that His Kingdom may come. What, again, will make that coming possible? By what means shall men become sure of God, how grow convinced that the doctrine of His Kingdom is true? There is only one way. They must do His will. "If any man shall do the will of God, he shall know of the doctrine, whether it be of God." "Not every one that saith unto Me, Lord, Lord, shall enter into the Kingdom of Heaven, but he that doeth the will." It is, then, in logical sequence to praying "Thy Kingdom come" that we pray next "Thy will be done." And thus the more closely we examine the structure of the Prayer, the more, I am sure, shall we discern its beauty and revere the wisdom which contrived it.

Perhaps some of us may need to guard ourselves against a misunderstanding of all this first part of the Lord's Prayer, which is, I think, rather common. To phrase it crudely, many people say the words in the sense of expressing a pious hope that God will work out His purposes, while mankind gratefully or submissively looks on. The idea of their petitions is that of asking God to cause His Name to be hallowed, and establish His Kingdom and do His will. But Divine power, by its own law, can do none of these things without the co-operation of human effort. These first sentences of the Paternoster are not just so many requests that things may be done. They are prayers that, with God's help, we may do things. We ask that that we, and our fellow-men, may hallow the name, that in and by us the Kingdom may come, that by us God's will may be done. And most of all, perhaps, in relation with the last of the three petitions does this truth need to be kept in mind. When people say, " God's will be done," they mean, as a rule, that if something they dislike is to befall them, they will try to bear it patiently. Although it is not what they would have chosen, nevertheless let God accomplish His purpose. There are special circumstances, no doubt, when this

may be a most right and noble prayer.
But, when made generally, it is apt to
give the effect of a bewildered and not
quite unresentful acquiescence. Of this
an unfortunate example is supplied by
a well-known hymn. Its suggestion—
which, obviously, its writer cannot have
intended—is that God multiplies mis-
fortunes on those that love Him; the
stanzas are a kind of catalogue of calami-
ties, and on each follows the refrain,
" Thy will be done." Much might be
said of the harm wrought by such teaching.
The one point, however, which concerns
us here is that it misunderstands strangely
the petition of the Lord's Prayer, which we
have now to consider. As Jesus taught
us to use them, the words " Thy will be
done " are not a prayer for passive
resignation. They are a prayer for active
service. They do not mean chiefly " May
God do His will," but " May we do God's
will." And we ask that we may do it,
not of constraint but of choice ; even as
the angels do it, not because they must,

76

but because they love. " As in heaven,
so on earth."

II

To be sure that we interpret rightly
this, as the other sentences of the Paternoster, we must needs turn not to any
author of hymns, not to any great saint
whose asceticism may have tinged the
Christian thought of his time, but to
the words and example of Jesus Himself.
And both these show that the supreme
purpose of His life was ever to do the will
of the Father. " My meat is to do the
will of Him that sent Me." " I seek not
mine own will, but the will of Him that
sent Me." " For I am come down from
heaven, not to do mine own will, but the
will of him that sent Me." With this
repeated emphasis He insists upon the
fact : " to do the will "—not merely to
bear, but to do—" of Him that sent Me "
is His own definition of His ministry.
And He bids men have the same aim :

that one shall be admitted to the Kingdom who " does the will of My Father " ; they who strive for it are recognized as His spiritual kindred : " Whosoever shall do the will of God, the same is my brother, and my sister, and mother."

As Christ thus plainly set before Himself the doing of the Father's will as His purpose, as he insisted repeatedly that the active doing of the will is the test of true discipleship, we may wonder how the sentence from his Prayer came to be misunderstood, and weakened into a profession of patient submission. The answer lies, no doubt, in the wrong sense people have attached to the words spoken in the garden of Gethsemane. " Not as I will, but as Thou wilt," He cried to the Father, and used again the very phrase He had taught others to use, " Thy will be done." This has been taken popularly to mean in effect, that, He desired the Father's purpose to be worked out, while the Son bowed to it submissively. Thus the sentence has been accounted a prayer for the spirit of patience, for fortitude to bear, for uncomplaining resignation. But this is, if not a quite false, at least a quite inadequate, view. When Jesus prayed " Thy will be done," in Gethsemane, He would not have ended the sentence " Thy will be done by Thee," but " Thy will be done by Me."

Then, with supreme resolve in that supreme hour, He bent Himself anew to the task. There was but a short space left before the Crucifixion, yet there were ways still in which the Father's will might be done. And it is well for us to notice what has been termed " the animation of our Lord's surrender," the passion of His Passion. He did not merely accept what came ; up to the very end He sought eagerly for opportunities of ministering, as the Father willed, to the souls of men. Even on the Cross there were murderers to be prayed for, and a penitent to be pardoned, and a mother to be sheltered, and at

79

the last He was able—as none else ever
has been able—to cry, " It is finished."
All was complete. The Father's will
was done.

III

Therefore the words and deeds of
Jesus show quite plainly what He had
in mind when He bade His disciples use
this sentence of His Prayer. They were
to ask that they might follow the rule
of life which had been His own, and
dedicate themselves without reserve to
doing the will of God. Through men
united by that aim would the Kingdom
come. We need often, and then may
ask fitly, a submissive spirit, resignation
to bear trials the reason of which lies
beyond our understanding. Yet in the
Paternoster that for which we ask God's
help is not that we may bear, but that we
may do ; that we may have insight to
recognize our opportunities of service
and strength to use them. The thought

could not be summarized better than it is in one of the Prayer-book collects, which asks for God's people " that they may both perceive and know what things they ought to do, and also may have grace and power faithfully to fulfil the same."

Nothing, perhaps, so helps us to measure the difference in scope and value between the " negative " and " positive " interpretations of this petition as to ponder the results could we attain in this stage the life of the prayer's perfect fulfilment. Were that achieved when " Thy will be done " is given its common " negative " meaning patience would be complete. There would be no murmuring against the decrees of Providence. We should bear readily whatever of strain or burden was imposed upon us by God. Ours would be that trusting spirit of submission for which our saying of the words is popularly supposed to ask. That would bring, no doubt, some real gain, provided that we did not ascribe to God sufferings actually due to our own fault or to the malignant powers of evil. At best, though, how small the gain would seem when set beside the fulfilment of "Thy will be done" in its positive sense! First, for our individual selves, it would mean that every one of us had an immensely simplified life. Every moment of it would be controlled by one law, the doing of God's will. We should care for this, and for nothing else. Thereby we should escape the tangle of rival motives, and achieve something of that serene tranquillity with which the unhurried Master moved from one day to another, from one task to the next. To be singly bent on doing the will of God is to know the secret of His composure.

Or, think, again, of the result on our common life. How vastly its quarrels and acerbities would be lessened! Differences of opinion, no doubt, would remain, due as they are to diversities of temperament and education and experience. But our social problems would be faced in a new spirit. In a sense, our "unhappy divisions," ecclesiastical or political, need not be unhappy at all, but rather a sign of life. Truth will ever remain greater than any one individual's, or party's, powers of perception; each will see some aspect which is invisible to others. The existence of "divisions," then, is a sign that our beliefs are honest, that we are trying to see as much as we can of truth for ourselves. What is "unhappy" is the spirit of rancour between those honestly divided, not the divisions themselves. And rancour must vanish between those, of views however divergent, who are united by a common effort to fulfil this petition of the Lord's Prayer.

Let us take a concrete example. Suppose—it needs a little imagination, unhappily—some great industrial dispute to be in progress. At length (it should be at the start) representatives of the two sides are brought together for conference. As things are now, probably each side is anxious for a victory, or, at best, for a settlement which keeps as much and gives as little as is necessary for some sort of workable compromise. But suppose that the representatives of the two parties met with the one desire, not to score a victory, not to patch up some kind of working compromise, but to do the will of God ? Suppose that their first act was to pray together " Thy will be done," and that then they set themselves resolutely to see how they could accomplish this ? It would remain for them, obviously, to decide what way God's will pointed, and often this would be interpreted at first with marked differences. But soon—incredibly soon, as the world would judge—those who had met in the spirit, had prayed together that they might do God's will, and had put aside all lower aims, would find themselves guided into agreement. This may seem a fantastic picture. There would be nothing impossible in it were ours in truth a Christian country, or even if all those who habitually pray " Thy will be done " felt and obeyed the real meaning of the words.

Imagine once more this same motive to control international councils, so that the question asked by each nation was not " How can we consolidate our realms ? " " How can we achieve security ? " " How can we foster our trade ? "—but, " How can we do God's will ? " Again a far-off vision ! Yet it is only along that road that the world will arrive at real peace, when the ideals of Christ are seen to be practical wisdom, when this sentence of the Lord's Prayer becomes not merely the aspiration of our lips, but the one purpose of our deeds, and with an earnestness undaunted by failures, no matter how many, we set ourselves to hallow God's Name, to build His Kingdom, and to do His will—on earth, even as in Heaven.

Chapter V

TO-MORROW'S BREAD

V. To-Morrow's Bread

I

WE have now to consider the second part of the Lord's Prayer: that which teaches us, having made petitions for God's glory, to add others about our human needs. Yet these sentences too must be unselfish; whatever we ask is not for our individual selves alone, but for all our fellow-men. Thus the prayer can never be inopportune. If there be any want made known by it which is not ours at the moment, we may be sure that it is felt acutely by myriads of others, and for them we intercede. And there is great comfort in the thought that we are encouraged by Jesus to speak thus to our Father; not merely to worship or to petition for the growth of His Kingdom, but to pray about our own human wants, and to be confident that

He will answer. It seems a fact of vast significance, not to be ignored even in the most scientific discussion of prayer and its efficacy, that He Who knew both human nature and the mind of God beyond all other should have been thus explicit in His certainty about prayer and its wide scope.

In considering the second part of the Paternoster, let us follow the same general lines as before, concerning ourselves less with remoter applications of the word than with the words themselves, and trying to elicit their exact meaning. I am sure that the need of this is greater than most of us, naturally enough, imagine.

Thus we may suppose that the first of these latter petitions, which we know in the form " Give us this day our daily bread," is of a significance quite self-evident. Yet, in point of fact, there is no other sentence of the Paternoster the true force of which has been the theme of such prolonged debate among scholars.

Its meaning depends upon the Greek word for which " daily " has been made to stand as the English equivalent. (This translation, as it happens, is really due to the Latin version of the Prayer, and not directly to the Greek.) But the original Greek word appears only in the Lord's Prayer—both in the Matthæan and Lucan versions. It occurs nowhere else in the Greek Testament, and, as yet, has been found in no other Greek writing. Within years comparatively recent our knowledge of the Greek New Testament has been increased vastly by the discovery among the papyri of many non-literary documents—such as private letters, notices, and bills—written in Greek of the same period.[1] Thus we have been helped to be sure about the meaning of words that appear only a few times in the New Testament, and not at all, or with other shades of meaning,

[1] The reader will find a "popular" and most fascinating account of this, and its bearing upon the New Testament, in Professor Milligan's volume, "Among the Papyri" (Hodder & Stoughton, Ltd.).

in earlier Greek. Thirty years ago there were about five hundred words which were supposed to belong to the special vocabulary of New Testament Greek, and were unknown outside it. Now, thanks to the papyri, the number has been reduced to about fifty. Moreover, we have learnt that the kind of Greek used in the New Testament was not, as had been thought, an artificial idiom, but was the common speech of the time. Many of the Jews were bilingual, like the modern Welsh, and spoke both Aramaic and Greek.

So far, however, this word, translated " daily," has not been discovered anywhere outside these two places in the New Testament—outside, that is, the two versions of the Lord's Prayer. Was it coined for the purpose, invented to render some special Aramaic word used by Jesus when He taught the Prayer ? Or, again, was it used by Him on some occasion when He spoke the Prayer in Greek ? This may be less likely, yet it is not impossible. The real point that concerns us, however, is to make ourselves as sure as we can of its actual meaning.

How is this to be done ? Well, let us imagine that in reading an English book we came upon a word new to us—a word, moreover, we could not find in any dictionary. What we should do would be to ponder its possible derivations. There might be more than one. Let us invent a word, to make the point clear. Let us fancy that we met the word " resignment "—which does not, I think, exist. What, we should ask, is its meaning ? Evidently something connected with " resigning." But then a further question must follow. Has it something to do with " resigning," " resignation," " giving up "—or is it connected with " re-signing," " adding another signature ? " That is a rough analogy to the kind of inquiry scholars have had to pursue with regard to the adjective attached to " bread " in the Paternoster.

Our Father

II

It would be needless to attempt even to summarize all the theories, but, in the main, two derivations have been thought possible. According to the former, the two words taken together would mean "bread for our being," "bread for our subsistence," and so "the bread we need." According to the other derivation they would mean "bread for the immediately coming time," "bread for the coming day," or, as we should put it in ordinary English, "bread for to-morrow." And it may be said, I think, that this latter interpretation is now supported by a majority—perhaps by a large majority—of modern scholars. Their decision is based, of course, on technical grounds, unsuitable for discussion here. But we shall see easily, I think, how welcome this decision is for reasons other than technical—how aptly it fits with the rest of our Lord's teaching, how greatly it enriches this sentence of the Lord's Prayer. Arranging the words as they stand in the original, the petition will be : " Our bread of to-morrow give us this day." Dr. Moffatt's rendering, in his version of St. Matthew vi. 11, is " Give us to-day our bread for the morrow."

We will assume, then, this to be the true meaning. And before noticing in detail how real is the gain which it brings, let us remark that there is no corresponding loss ; that the force of the petition as we have used it hitherto still remains. The main thought, doubtless, which the words " Give us this day our daily bread " held for us has been that we look to God for the things (in the Prayer-book phrase) " requisite and necessary as well for the body as the soul " ; that our bodily needs are not forgotten by our Father, and that we have Christ's authority for praying about them. The new rendering leaves us still the welcome comfort of that truth. As much as ever our sense of dependence on God is emphasized. Yet the precise point of emphasis is changed. The old thought, though retained in its fullness, becomes subsidiary to the new. In its chief significance the prayer becomes one less for food than for peace of mind. The reason of our asking for the food is that we may be freed from anxiety. " Give us— not accumulated wealth, not heaped-up stores for all the days to come—we do not ask for that—but give us sufficient simple provender in hand that our lives may not be marred by over-anxiety about the morrow. Give us to-day to-morrow's bread."

Let us think of the people to whom first our Lord taught this prayer—the people amongst whom He lived and worked. A few of them were rich. A few were so poor as to be almost destitute. But the most of them were, as we should say, people of narrow means. So long as they could earn their wages they managed well enough. Only there was nothing to spare. They had no margin. The day's wage had to buy the day's food. If an unexpected guest arrived, there would be nothing in the cupboard; the host must try to borrow some provision from a neighbour. With people so circumstanced, one of the worst troubles, affecting their whole thought and making them less easily reached by any spiritual message, was this uncertainty about the necessaries of life, this so frequent worry about to-morrow's food. The Gospels show that our Lord found it a real obstacle to His mission. It engrossed the hearts of men, so that they were slow to receive His message. It precluded that serene tranquillity of mind which was His own, which He longed to impart to His followers. They were apt to be absorbed by the task of obtaining " the meat which perisheth," by their material wants. Our Lord tried to combat this influence. He spoke about it explicitly, urging His listeners to master over-anxiety about the morrow, this worry over obtaining food and drink and clothes.

But He gave them His sympathy too, for He Himself had known want, and had felt the downward pull of material needs. He understood how hard it was for them to heed spiritual teaching unless they could be liberated from this worry, by knowing that they had something in hand. So He encouraged them to pray for it, and to ask that God would remove their need for anxiety by letting them possess enough for the morrow. " Give us to-day," they were to pray, " to-morrow's bread."

III

If this be the true meaning of the sentence, it is ~~not~~ one we shall value highly. As the first of the petitions we are taught to make for ourselves, we ask to be made, not wealthy, but sure of the morrow, exempt from the mental troubles which militate fiercely against the life of the soul. And the presence of this clause in the Lord's Prayer shows that He sympathizes with us about this. He knows the evil influence of worry, on soul and body alike. Worry kills more people in this country each year than does influenza or any other plague.

Experience confirms, too, the understanding wisdom shown in the wording of the sentence. It is not so much the present difficulty that is so hard to bear as the less definite troubles about the future, the absence of a margin, the fears about to-morrow's bread. Probably this trial was never more common than in our own age, with its financial stringency and unsettled outlook. We find it in many walks of life. Here—to take instances almost at random—is a workingman ; he has a job at the moment, but is afraid of being turned adrift to-morrow. Here is a journalist who has served his paper through long years. He has given it his best. But there are rumours of a changed proprietorship and many dismissals ; his heart is sick with fear about to-morrow's bread. Here is a clerk, on an income which makes saving impossible. His employers talk of forced economies, through the decline of trade, and a reduced staff. What, he wonders, is to become then of his delicate wife and children ? Or the writer with a dwindling market, or a minor actress near the end of a run, or the elderly governess, or the professional worker with increasing expenses and diminishing income. . . . Were it an actually present trouble, of which they knew the worst, it would be easier to bear, in a sense, than this harassing uncertainty about the future. They live their lives bravely, they try to hope for the best ; few of their friends and none of their acquaintances are allowed to guess that they are haunted by this spectre of anxiety. Yet there are solitary moments in the dark of night when the burden seems almost greater than they can bear. Had they only, as we say, something to fall back upon, had they some little store in hand, their whole prospect would be transformed.

Or here (to take an instance of a quite different kind) is a statesman gravely concerned over perils which, in his judgment, the nation will have to face before long. Its resources are enough, perhaps, to meet immediate needs—but will they suffice for that morrow ?

IV

I need not multiply examples. Do we not know, in some degree, these fears about our future, or about the futures of those we love ? And, when it becomes acute, this anxiety preys not only upon physical but upon spiritual health. It becomes extraordinarily difficult for people to lift their thoughts to the highest things while they are obsessed by these haunting worries, and have nothing in hand. It is this that they crave—to have some security, to feel that, whatever to-morrow's need, they have provision for it safe in store. " Give us to-day," they ask, "to-morrow's bread!" It seems a thought to be treasured that when we use this sentence of the Lord's Prayer we are praying for all these people, the anxious and heavy laden; all the brave folk who carry on stoutly, yet at heart are dismayed by the fear of a breadless morrow —dismayed, likely enough, far less for themselves than for the sake of wife, or husband, or children. As we understood the words in the past, we prayed in this clause of the Paternoster for bodily needs alone. "Give us the bread we need to-day." As this other rendering interprets it, we pray for tranquillity of mind as well as for bodily food; in fact, our reason for asking that we may have the necessaries of bodily life in advance is that thereby we may secure peace of mind. And we ask for peace of mind because a disquieted mind wars against the life of the soul.

When we think again of the humble folk to whom first our Lord gave His Prayer, we can understand how readily they would welcome the use the sentence which prayed to-day for to-morrow's bread. The question had been asked, however, whether to take the petition in this sense be not discrepant with our Lords exhortation to " take no thought for the morrow." Yet the answer is simple. The command was not really to take no thought for the morrow, but as the Revised version rightly indicates, " be not anxious," "be not over anxious," " do not worry " about to-morrow And then in the Lord's Prayer He bids us pray for what will remove the cause of over-anxiety. Indeed, the best safeguard against it is to cast our cares upon God, to bring our wants for the morrow before Him in prayer.

And the prayer is heard. In ways past finding out, in ways past man's understanding, God does supply the needs of those who trust Him. Theirs (the history of a myriad disciples confirms the fact) is a tranquillity of mind which has grown out of experience. For each coming day God makes provision beforehand, until the last—and beyond the last. He will give us to-day, in this sense also, to-morrow's bread ; will bestow now the strength we shall need when this day is done. To the life spent apart from God the evening comes chill and disconsolate : the shadows thicken as the end seems near. To the life with God also evening comes—yet it is no ending of life. Faith feels the night-wind, and knows it for the herald of fresh youth. Faith views the tranquil sundown, and sees in its last glow a promise of the leaping dawn.

CHAPTER VI

FORGIVENESS

VI. *Forgiveness* ❧ ❧ ❧

I

THERE are some slight but interesting differences of wording in the
petition for forgiveness as recorded in
the First and Third Gospels. St. Matthew's version, literally rendered, is :

> Forgive us our debts,
> As we also have forgiven our debtors ;

and St. Luke's :

> Forgive us our sins,
> For we ourselves forgive every one indebted
>   to us.

Another interesting variant is that of the
Old Syriac version, which seems often to
reproduce the original Aramaic with
special fidelity. In place of the Mat-

thæan "we have forgiven," or the Lucan
" we forgive," it has " we will forgive."
According to the First Gospel, those using
the Prayer say that they have forgiven
already; according to the Third, that
they forgive habitually, and in the Syriac
version they promise that they will forgive. With all, obviously, the sense is
practically identical; in each he who
uses the Prayer accepts the condition on
which our Lord insisted often, that we
may not ask forgiveness of God unless
we ourselves are ready to forgive our
fellow-men. Such slight variations may
represent, as we have seen already, slightly
differing forms of the Prayer as taught by
our Lord at different times. But the
Matthæan " debts " seems more probably
the equivalent of what He said than the
Lucan " sins." This evangelist himself
has " debtors " in the second half of the
sentence, and we may feel sure that the
thought of the two parts—" our debts,"
" our debtors " would correspond. " Forgiveness of sins " was a phrase so constantly

used in New Testament and other early Christian writings that we can easily understand how it would come naturally to mind and be written down in place of forgiveness of " debts." Yet our conviction that " debts," used by St. Matthew, more probably represents the word used by our Lord Himself in teaching the Prayer is strengthened when we recollect other passages in which he enforced the same truth. Particularly we shall remember the parable of the Two Debtors—of the man who was forgiven a debt of pounds but would not forgive a debt of pence.

Again, it may be thought that the difference of meaning between " sins " and " debts " is not important. The Greek word rendered " sins " means literally " a missing of the mark," so that " going astray " or " trespass " represents it accurately. The word rendered " debt " means, when not used figuratively, a literal " money-debt," and has been found in this sense in various papyri. It is

true, of course, that all " sin " is, in some
some degree, a failure to pay our just
debts to God—our debt of obedience,
our debt of gratitude. Yet I incline to
think that there is a distinction, and that
when Jesus bade us pray " forgive us
our debts " His choice of this word shows
Him to have meant particularly what are
termed " faults of omission." These, in
the strict sense, are debts to God which
we have failed to pay.

For it was upon these that He laid most
stress in His doctrine. To regain its
force, we must needs remember how
amazingly novel it seemed to the people
of His time. His standards and values
differed widely from those of their accredited religious teachers. These, it
is true, described " righteousness " as
man's supreme aim, and the casual listener
might hear this new Rabbi also extolling
" righteousness," and therefore following
apparently, the accustomed lines. But
as he heard more, he discovered " with
increasing astonishment " (such is the

precise meaning of the word used by the Evangelists) that the content of our Lord's teaching, the ideas He held about the nature of " righteousness," were wholly new. In particular—this is the point which concerns us here—He seemed to be grieved by what men abstained from doing rather than by what they did.

With us it has become a truism that His positive teaching contrasted with the Rabbi's negative morality, that His " thou shalt " replaced the old " thou shalt not." Yet even now it may be doubted if we have made our moral code approximate to that of Jesus, or really have adopted His scale of values, His categories of right and wrong. He made astonishingly little of what were reckoned serious offences ; the omissions, the failures to use opportunities of doing good were the faults He condemned unsparingly. He put before His hearers a tremendous picture of a final judgment ; its setting was reproduced, to a great extent, from Apocalyptic writings, but its appraisals of conduct were emphatically new. And in that picture, as we shall remember, the hapless condemned " at the left hand " were not they who, in the common phrase, " had done wrong," but they who had failed to do right—they who wilfully had missed opportunities for kindness, for comforting, for helping, for shewing love to their neighbours.

Therefore it is strictly consonant with the rest of His teaching that His prayer bids us ask that we may be forgiven not for the wrong things we have done, but for the right things we have failed to do ; not " forgive us our trespasses," but " forgive us our debts." Our trespasses also need forgiveness, beyond doubt. Yet He might suppose that, without prompting, we should seek God's pardon for these, while we are apt to think of less account, or to ignore entirely, those faults of omission which in fact are far more serious. Many a conscience is not seriously perturbed as it reviews the definitely wrong actions of which it has cognizance. Without undue boasting, a great many people are able to feel that —if only through the circumstances of their lives, their upbringing, and their freedom from the grosser temptations— they have been able to keep themselves comparatively free from what are commonly thought of as really base forms of moral turpitude. Their lapses (for which they are quite ready to ask the Divine forgiveness) have not been, they feel, very numerous. On the whole, they do not seem to themselves to have done a great deal of wrong. But how this complacency crumbles away if they come to apprehend Christ's view, and reckon the loss of each opportunity for doing good as real sin ! How innumerable are the debts to God and our neighbour—and to God through our neighbour—we have failed to pay ! And it is these—these lost opportunities, it seems—which Jesus thought the most serious of all failings. Does not that truth drive home to us our need of forgiveness ?

Therefore, if we retain the familiar form of words and say " Forgive us our trespasses " when we repeat the Paternoster, we shall not use the sentence rightly unless we remember its true meaning, given in the Bible version of the Prayer, " forgive us our debts "—remission of debts left unpaid, forgiveness for missed opportunities, for kind words and deeds unsaid and undone. " Forgive us our debts ! "

II

To remember this meaning will add also to the poignancy which the second clause of the petition has for us. In practice it is the " debts," owed to us but unpaid, that we find hardest to forgive our neighbour. No doubt, if we think that he has done us a definite wrong by word or deed, the task of forgiving him from our hearts is none too easy. Yet easier it is than to forgive those who have made no effort to pay what we had every right to expect. Perhaps we have done much for them. We have a substantial claim on their gratitude. But when in turn we need their help, when a little kindness or sympathy from them would mean much, and we, who have relied upon it, find that it is withheld—then the sense of injury rankles, and we do not find it easy to forgive these debtors of ours. "As we also have forgiven our debtors" is probably a more difficult word to say with full sincerity than "as we forgive them that trespass against us." But it must be said, if we are to ask that our own debts to God be remitted.

If we wonder why Jesus seemed to view as so far more heinous the faults of omission than those of commission, the reason does not seem beyond our understanding. We may remember that many of the deeds condemned by popular opinion as the worst sins were offences, in part, against a real moral law, but in part also merely against a sociological code, with a basis human rather than

divine. To neglect a chance of kindness
on the contrary, was, in the view of
Christ, to sin against the law of love—
far more important, in His view, than
any other. Again, we shall be helped to
understand His judgment when we remember the view of God bestowed by
Him, and emphasized in the first words
of this Prayer. It is addressed to " our
Father." There is no fault of children
which pains a father so deeply as ingratitude. Let us imagine the instance of
two sons ; one of them gets into some
foolish entanglement, or runs up bills
extravagantly. He has done wrong, yet
him the father, remembering the temptations of his own hot youth, will find it
not very difficult to forgive. The other
is a pattern of outward decorum. But he
is self-centred and selfish. His father,
being unwell, hopes that this son will
keep him company for a few days. He
does not suggest it, longing that the son
should propose it himself. But the son
departs, having a more lively engagement

elsewhere. He gives never a thought to all that the father has done for him, the self-sacrifice which provided a good education; he makes no attempt at all to repay even a little of this debt of kindness. He ignores it with bland complacency. Will not the father find this attitude much harder to forgive than the other son's lapses from virtue, be grieved far more by the one's faults of omission than by the other's faults of commission ? And as God's relation with us (so Jesus taught) is that of a loving father with his children, do we not get a glimpse of the manner in which He must sorrow over our terrible lack of gratitude, our so frequent forgetfulness of all we owe to him ? Thinking of this, we seem to understand why our Lord has taught us in His Prayer to say, " Forgive us our debts."

Perhaps a word should be added about the second part of the sentence. When we pray " Forgive us . . . as we forgive," clearly that does not mean a request that the Divine forgiveness shall be merely proportionate to ours. Ill would it be for us were there, so to speak, an exact scale of reciprocity, if the pardon we may hope to receive could not exceed the pardon we were able to bestow. We know that our unpaid debts to God are vastly greater than any owed to us by our fellow-men. St. Luke's version of the Prayer safeguards us against such misunderstanding. It replaces " as " by " for," so that unmistakably the petition is not " forgive us *in proportion as* we forgive," but " forgive us *because* we forgive." When we use the words, we affirm that we are trying to fulfil the condition which justifies us in asking forgiveness. We may try imperfectly, yet at least we try. Before we can make the petition for ourselves we must try to let the spirit of charity and forgiveness take possession of our hearts. So shall we put ourselves in tune with God, and be made ready to ask, without unfitness, for His pardon.

Then, indeed, we are certain of gaining it. For the actions of God, as Jesus taught, are not arbitrary and capricious. They are controlled immutably by His own law. Therefore it is no mere matter of speculation whether or no God remits our debts. Two conditions must be fulfilled. There must be real "repentance" for our failures—which means no mere emotional regret but a steadfast purpose to do better. And there must be the spirit of forgiveness towards our debtors. Let these two things be present, and we can ask forgiveness in full certainty that the prayer will be answered. So prayed, it must gain its end, by God's perpetual law.

III

An attempt to study in full our Lord's teaching about forgiveness would take us too far from our present theme. Yet to understand and use rightly these words of the Paternoster will set us free from misunderstandings that are strangely common. People still speak as though the Master had enjoined a forgiveness quite indiscriminate. His words show how false an idea is this. For one thing we are to be ready to forgive the wrong-doer whenever he shall show penitence, but not before; " if thy brother sin against thee and he repent, forgive him," is the command; if our forgiveness is to be moulded upon God's, then we know that to forgive while there was exultant persistence in wrong-doing would be no act of true love. And, for another thing, it is not wrongs in general, still less wrongs done to others, but wrongs done to ourselves only, which we are to be ready to forgive. Not—reverting for a moment to the familiar rendering of the Prayer—" as we forgive them that trespass," but strictly " them that trespass *against us*." Other injuries must be left to another judgment. Only when we ourselves have suffered have we ourselves the duty and honour of forgiving.

Such is the spirit, then, in which we shall make this petition; mindful of our illimitable failures, our ingratitude, our swiftness to judge others harshly. "Forgive us our debts. And this we ask, resolute ourselves to forgive our debtors."

Chapter VII

TEMPTATION AND EVIL

VII. *Temptation and Evil* ͻ

" NOT into temptation." . . .
Concerning these words much
has been written, for the sentence in
which they stand has ever been accounted
the most difficult of the Lord's Prayer.
But the point of difficulty has shifted
within modern times, so that of the newer
problem there seems to be still something
which needs to be said. True, neither
the child at a mother's knee nor the aged
cottager repeating the Prayer will stray
far from the essential meaning. Each,
at least, knows temptation ; each asks
to be delivered from evil. Rightly, however, we desire more than a general
idea of the significance which the sentence
possesses. The more closely we examine
the Paternoster, the more spiritually
vital it becomes ; the more our eyes are

opened to the wealth of teaching beneath
the simplicity of phrase. And it is, I
believe, by a close scrutiny of the exact
wording that we may hope to solve the
problems and arrive at the true force of
this final petition in the Lord's Prayer.

Of the older and more familiar difficulty
little, perhaps, need be said now, but it
seems to have been felt keenly in the
earlier days of the Christian Church.
" Are we to believe," men asked, " that
God leads us into temptation ? If so,

> O Thou, who didst with pitfall and with gin
> Beset the Road I was to wander in,
> Thou wilt not with Predestin'd Evil round
> Enmesh, and then impute my Fall to Sin ! "

We shrink from such a thought—yet
how else is it needful, as Jesus teaches, to
beseech the Father that he will not lead
us into temptation ? From very early
times some people had tried to excuse
their misdeeds by assigning the blame to
God, and the son of Sirach reproved them :

" Say not thou : It is through the Lord
that I fell away. . . . Say not thou :
It is He that caused me to err." Afterwards St. James repeated the warning,
in his own blunt fashion : " Let no man
say when he is tempted : I am tempted
of God." Was he driven to enforce
this because already the sentence of the
Paternoster had been misunderstood, and
mischievous arguments based on the misunderstanding ? In later years we may
be sure that the difficulty was increased
by the rendering of the Greek phrase
by " ne nos *inducas* " in Latin, and,
from the Latin, by " *Lead* us not " in
English. Those words would be the
right equivalent of another Greek verb
than that which is used ; in the one
actually employed there is no such strong
directive sense. The Revised Version
has recognized this by putting " Bring
us not " in place of " Lead us not,"
and we might wish that " Bring us not "
were adopted in our liturgical use of
the Prayer. Yet that change, though

it would lessen, would not remove the difficulty—the difficulty of supposing the words to imply that God, unless our prayers intervened, might bring man into temptation.

The way to the right understanding of them seems to be shown by some variants of the sentence—Dr. Chase has shown that they were both very ancient and very widespread. Indeed, these " glosses " often passed from liturgical versions of the Prayer, where, in all probability, they originated, into actual texts of the Matthæan and Lucan Gospels. The most felicitous, perhaps, is that quoted by St. Augustine : " Many people when using the Prayer word this sentence ' Suffer us not to be led into temptation.' " (*Multi precando ita dicunt : Ne nos patiaris induci in tentationem.*) This turn of the sentence, given it in very early times, persisted through centuries, and passed, indeed, into our own tongue. As I write, I have before me a copy, printed in 1542, of " A Necessary Doctrine and Erudition

for any Christian man, set furthe by the
Kynges majestie of Englande." We may
suppose Cranmer, rather than Henry VIII,
to have been its actual author. Among
its contents is an exposition of the Paternoster. First the Prayer is printed in
full, and then each of its clauses, with
explanations. All the other sentences
stand exactly as we know and use them,
but this follows the variations mentioned
by St. Augustine, and—alike in the text
of the Prayer and commentary—is worded:
" And let us not be ledde into temptation."

Mere gloss though it be, we can hardly
doubt that this expansion of the original
sentence reveals its true meaning.
Naturally enough, the Greek sentence—
probably like the Aramaic it translated—
was phrased as concisely as possible,
that it might be memorized the more
easily. And, for the same reason, a
parallelism of form would be preserved
between it and the petitions which
preceded it. Thus " bring us not into

temptation " is a condensed sentence, so to speak ; is an example of what the grammarians call " brachyology." But the spirit of the petition it makes is " Suffer us not to be brought into temptation." When thus understood and used, the older difficulty associated with it disappears.

II

But another, and a far more serious, difficulty survives for the thoughtful disciple of modern days. Recognizing that the words contain no suggestion that we might be "tempted of God," discerning " suffer us not to be brought into temptation " as their true meaning, he is driven yet to ask why we are taught to make this prayer. It seems to ask the impossible. We are sure that Jesus never bade his disciples to offer petitions which, from their very nature, could never be fulfilled. Yet such a petition would be one asking that we might

escape temptation. Not the greatest
saint that ever lived could be exempt from
it. Nor for our Lord Himself in His
earthly life was this possible. And we
are not to suppose that His only temptations were those He faced in solitude
immediately after the Baptism. There
were others which beset Him throughout
His ministry, and some at least—perhaps
the temptation to abandon His work in
the face of hostility and seeming failure
—He bore in common with His
disciples. "Ye are they," He said to
them near the end, "which have con-
tinued with Me in My temptations."
How, then, can we ask to be spared that
which is, in fact, inevitable? Why should
we seem to ask for escape from the common
lot of human nature? What do we really
mean when we say, "Lead us not into
temptation"?

A commentator of the older school
cites the words as an example of our
Lord's "idealism." We are told that
"as He commanded His disciples to be

perfect, though knowing well that perfection far exceeded their reach, so here He bids them pray for the ideal state, for freedom from all temptation, although in this world the prayer cannot be completely answered." The reader will agree, I think, that this is a most unsatisfying explanation. It is one thing to propound an ideal standard of human conduct ; it is quite another to implore God daily to grant what, in point of fact, we know He cannot grant. Moreover—and here we touch the heart of the difficulty—" freedom from temptation " would *not* be " the ideal state " for human beings in this world. To desire it would be, speaking bluntly, the height of foolishness, would be to ignore all that God has revealed concerning moral growth.

For we have learnt no longer to confuse temptation with sin. We see that the potential good of temptation is as real as its potential evil. We understand how fundamental is the law of effort as the condition of all progress. Science has taught us to discern its operation in the physical world, and to see struggle crowned by survival in the cosmic evolutionary process. And in the spiritual world also it is he who overcometh that inheriteth. To meet and to master temptation seems to be the one means of strengthening character, so that did we not meet temptation we could make no moral progress. Even for our Lord Himself, being Man, the rule held. It could be only His conquest over temptation which caused Him, in St. Luke's bold phrase, " to grow in favour with God." And, though temptation was of the devil, it was by the Spirit that He was led to meet it. In short, so far as we can understand, if human nature were debarred from meeting temptation, it would be debarred also from the possibility of moral growth. St. James may have had this truth in mind when he wrote a sentence which our English Bible—both Authorized and Revised Versions— gravely mistranslates. Whatever its exact force, St. James did not mean to say, " Count it all joy when ye fall *into* divers temptations." What he did say was (literally) that Christians should be glad " when ye fall [i.e. from tranquil well-being] so as to be compassed about by manifold trials." The " trials " of this sentence, however, may be external rather than internal ; " afflictions," " persecutions," rather than moral temptations.

Here, however, our concern is with the words " Bring us not "—or " Suffer us not to be brought "—" into temptation." To pray that we may escape meeting temptation, so far from being a petition in keeping with the rest of the Lord's Prayer, would be both futile and foolish. It would be futile, because, this could not be granted ; it would be foolish, for if it were granted it would be to our hurt. How, then, are we to interpret, in what sense are we to use, this sentence of the Paternoster ? The answers supplied by commentaries are various, yet alike in being forced, elaborate, and therefore unsatisfying. Often an attempt is made to distinguish between " normal " temptations and " extra and avoidable " temptations, and to argue that this petition is restricted to the latter. Thus, in his volume on the Sermon on the Mount, Dr. Edward Lyttelton paraphrases the sentence : " May it not become necessary that we be roused from spiritual sloth by being brought into special temptation and so falling into sin." That is an explanation which rather needs explanation. It seems to imply that the Divine way of remedying our spiritual sloth is to cause us to fall into sin. But, apart from any such special point, this is one of the many explanations which are far too subtle and intricate. They seem to forget that the Prayer was given originally for use by the simple peasant and fisher folk of Galilee. Surely it is incredible that, among the very concise, lucid, and definite petitions of His model Prayer, our Lord should have introduced one that could be understood only if its words were construed in an abnormal sense, one that could be made intelligible only by an elaborate and arbitrary paraphrase.

Yet it seems nearly as impossible to disregard the precise wording, as Bishop Gore bids us, and " to interpret the prayer more generally as an expression of self-distrust." That, no doubt, it is. Yet it cannot be merely to express our self-distrust that we are bidden to pray "Bring us not into temptation," especially when we remember that only by meeting temptation can we gain strength. Would our Lord wish our self-distrust to be expressed by asking that we should miss the one experience which makes spiritual growth possible ? No ; the explanation of these so simple and direct words must itself be direct and simple. It must lie within the words themselves, not in misty implications which may be drawn from them. And such an explanation seems ready to our hand.

III

The petition is that we may not be brought *into* temptation. That is quite different from a petition that we may not be brought *unto* temptation. As if to stress the point, the preposition is duplicated in Greek, in a way that cannot be reproduced in English ; " do not into-bring us into temptation " would be its literal equivalent. And, as the standard lexicon of New Testament Greek reminds us, this preposition " after verbs of going, coming, leading, etc., is joined to nouns designating the condition or state into which one passes," as of entering " into the Kingdom of God," " into life," " into punishment," and so forth. English readers miss this important shade of meaning in the Greek idiom. In Greek the movement " into " denotes a change for the person approaching not merely of outward position but of inward condition. To " enter into " the King-

dom of God is much more than to stand
within the Kingdom ; it is to yield to
its claims, to be dominated by it, to take
its law as the law of one's being. A
valediction which our Lord used often
does not mean, as English readers are
to suppose, " depart, and let your mind
be at peace," but " enter thou into the
state, or condition, of peace." And so
to " enter into " temptation is very
different from merely encountering temptation ; it is to yield to its demands, to
be subjugated by it.

Our Lord gives us no encouragement
to ask that we may not be brought *to*
temptation—a prayer, as we have reflected
which would be both futile and foolish.
But he does bid us pray that we may not
enter *into* it. When in Gethsemane
He bade His disciples " watch and pray,
that ye enter not into temptation," He
knew that within a few minutes temptation would confront them—the temptation of cowardice and disloyalty. For
them to ask that they might not be

brought *to* that temptation would have been useless. But He would have them desire that they might not be brought *into* it, into its power so as to be mastered by it. They must needs approach its walls, where the battle was to be fought. But they need not be led captive into its citadel.

This interpretation of the prayer seems to be confirmed by the remainder of the sentence. It is not an independent petition ; the separate petitions of the Paternoster are linked by the word " and." Here there is no " and " followed by a fresh petition ; " but deliver us from evil" merely completes and illuminates the prayer " bring us not into temptation." The Greek words at the close may mean either " from evil " or " from the evil one " ; on the whole, I think the impersonal rendering, as we have it in the familiar English version of the Prayer, gives us better sense. The point is, however, not of great importance. But we ought to notice carefully the preceding words. Those translated " deliver us " mean literally " draw us away to Thyself," and the preposition is " from," not " out of " evil. Therefore the force of the whole cannot be, as some have supposed, " Suffer us, so far as possible, not to be led into temptation ; but when, through our inevitable frailty, we have been led into it, help us to escape again out of its evil." Rather we ask that, when brought to temptation, we may not be brought into it, but may be saved from that entrance by the power of God, drawing us back from the evil to Himself.

Let us use a prosaic illustration to make the point clear. A man whose special weakness is drink has daily to pass a public-house on his way home from work. There is, we will imagine, no alternative road. So it would be vain to ask that he should not be brought to temptation. It stands on his way ; he cannot escape encountering it. But we can pray that he may not be brought into it ; that he may pass by the door without entering. And each time God's power enables him to do that he will be not a worse but a better man, because he has come to temptation without coming into it ; he will be the more likely to conquer again next time.

Thus we seem to have reached an interpretation of this sentence in our Lord's Prayer, derived from a study of its actual wording, which is simple, which satisfies, which clears away the difficulties and misunderstandings. No more need we deem ourselves bidden to intercede vainly that temptation may be wholly withheld from us. Satanic as is its source and fearful as are its perils, God's overruling power has utilized it as a means of our schooling in this stage of life Only by meeting temptation can we follow in our Master's steps, and, conquering through His power, make our characters rise nearer to His ideal. " Lead us not into temptation, but deliver us from evil ! " Daily we must come to temptation, yet " suffer us not," we ask, as He has taught, " to be brought, not merely to, but into

temptation, so that we pass into its heart
its power, its thrall; daily we must be
brought to temptation, but reinforce our
wills with Thy strength so that we may
resist and not be drawn over the threshold
into it; daily we must be brought to
temptation, but, O God, deliver us from
its evil!"

Chapter VIII

USING THE PRAYER

VIII. *Using the Prayer*   *   *

I

HERE, then, is the Lord's Prayer, as we have studied it:

Our Father in heaven!
As in heaven, so on earth
> Thy Name be reverenced,
> Thy Kingdom come,
> Thy will be done.

> Give us to-day to-morrow's bread.
> And forgive us our debts, for we forgive our debtors.
> And bring us not into temptation, but deliver us from evil.

No one could propose that we should substitute a new wording for that which we learnt in the nursery, which binds English-speaking folk the world over, which has been treasured by our forefathers through many generations. Yet we may be helped by remembering a more exact rendering, and by reading its sense into the older form as we use it. For we want the mind, as well as the heart, to strengthen the life of the soul. There were ages when the Lord's Prayer was popularly regarded as a kind of magical spell. To say—or to gabble—as many Paternosters as possible at full speed was an imagined means of averting punishment or of winning God's favour. If to-day we are exempt from superstition of that type, the danger of giving the Prayer but a formal and frigid repetition remains, with a vague idea that the mere " saying " of the Prayer is an act of virtue. Yet it is not enough to admire, or study, or say the Prayer, which was given us to be prayed. And so we have need to think not only of what Jesus taught us to pray, but of what He taught us about praying.

Originally, the Paternoster was meant, beyond doubt, for use in private ; only after a century or more does it seem to have found a place in the public worship of the Church. Our Lord's example, as well as His teaching, showed the importance He gave to private colloquy with the Father. He took part in public worship at synagogue and Temple, yet this could not suffice His needs without private prayer. Solitude was no easy thing for Him to secure through the years of His ministry. Most of those He addressed could do His bidding, and go into an inner chamber and shut the door when they would be alone with God. But for months together our Lord had no fixed home. One of the trials in His life which we are apt to overlook was this difficulty of getting away from people, of finding place for solitary thought and meditation and communion with God. We see Him bent upon achieving it, making determined efforts to get free from the crowd; instead of taking rest at the end of some tremendous day's work, making His tired way to the mountain or wilderness in order to gain, at any cost, that solitude for private prayer which His soul needed.

II

How in our own private devotions are we to make best use of the Prayer given us by the Master? First, we need not suppose ourselves constrained as by law to use it whenever we pray. Many, perhaps most, of those who pray regularly will like always to give it the foremost place in their devotions. But others may be helped to say it with greater intensity of meaning if they use it less often— perhaps at night only, or even more occasionally. "How" we say matters so much more than "how often" we say it. And at least whenever we detect ourselves saying it mechanically, or with a wandering mind, on the instant we should stop, and begin it afresh. Some people may find when the edge of the Prayer seems blunted, so to speak, that it can be revived by studying afresh each sentence in turn. Thus the address and the six petitions might be divided among the seven days of a week. On the first, in place of saying the whole Prayer, we should limit ourselves to " Our Father which art in Heaven," and think of God's heavenly perfection, of His relation with us as Father, of our duties as children. Next day we should try by quiet thought to draw out the meaning of " Hallowed be Thy Name," and so on through the other days. By the end of the week, possibly enough, the Lord's Prayer may mean more to us than ever it did before.

Whether or no we adopt this plan, I am certain that, as the Lord's Prayer was given in the first place for private use, we are meant to link with it our individual needs. Most writers of devotional books, from Lancelot Andrewes downwards, have included in their works one or more " paraphrases " of the Lord's Prayer, and none is better, perhaps, than that in

Andrewes' "Preces Privatæ." But any such general paraphrase made by another cannot suit exactly our own individual needs. We shall find it far better to make, each one of us, his own paraphrase. That is to say, we shall expand every petition of the Lord's Prayer by applying its words to our special circumstances. For instance, having said "Thy Kingdom come," I may well pause to think of ways by which I can help the coming of God's Kingdom, both in my own life and among other people within my influence. Or, after "Forgive us our debts" it will be very profitable for me to make myself face the chances I have missed of late, the right things left undone, and then, naming these specific debts, to ask God's forgiveness of them. That is less easy, and far more humiliating, than merely to own in general terms that I have failed and deplore the fact. But it is also vastly better for me, and gives my prayer far more reality.

Perhaps we shall find ourselves helped

towards being definite if we put our thoughts into spoken words, though they are to be heard by God alone. It seems to have been our Lord's habit so to speak aloud His private prayers. Thus He did in Gethsemane ; thus He did immediately before giving the Lord's Prayer. " It came to pass, as He was praying in a certain place, that when He ceased, one of His disciples said unto Him : Lord, teach us to pray." Probably we shall the more easily concentrate our thoughts if we follow His example. Of course there can be no fixed rule about this or other details of method—whether, for instance, we kneel or stand to pray. What matters is that we should take trouble, and find out what method suits us best, and try to learn how to pray better and better.

III

So far, we have thought of the use of the Paternoster in private prayer for our own individual needs. But we must not limit it to this purpose ; often we shall use it wholly as an act of intercession for others. When we were considering the petition " Give us to-day to-morrow's bread " we remarked upon the bitter need to-day of this prayer. And we should say the words at times with special thought of those out of work, and those enduring genteel poverty, and the multitudes, near and far, to whom the doubt concerning the morrow's bread is so crushing a burden. Again, at times we may use the Prayer with special intention. Suppose, for example, that we resolve to say it with particular reference to the work of God's Church on earth, we may be astonished to find how aptly each of its sentences seems to chime with some evident need of the Church to-day. And this is but one instance. The better we understand the Prayer, the more often we shall find that it expresses the intercession for various causes which we desire to make.

Using the Prayer

We shall remember, too, however frequent our use of the Paternoster, that it was not given to dispense us from the task of framing prayers of our own. On the contrary, its purpose was explicitly to encourage us in making these prayers, and to supply us with a pattern to copy. "After this manner pray ye." However limited our powers, we can try to imitate the qualities most characteristic of it. We can place God's glory before our own needs. We can make our prayers unselfish. Remembering its extreme brevity, we need not be concerned if we find it hard to pray for any length of time with that deep intensity of purpose which brings us near to God. We shall not repeat the error of those who thought they should be heard "for their much speaking." The prayers we make for ourselves will be utterly different from the Lord's Prayer in form and idiom; we should not try, indeed, to phrase them in an archaic style. But so far as their spirit is akin to that of the supreme model, so far shall we be praying " after the manner " that our Lord desires.

IV

There remains a further use, of a kind wholly different, to which we may put the Lord's Prayer. We may welcome its influence to strengthen our faith. The better we know it, the greater will become its marvel; the more certain we shall feel that no merely human teacher bequeathed it to the world. Let us recall once more its origin. A group of Jewish peasants clustered about Him Whom they supposed a Rabbi, and their spokesman asked Him to do as the Baptist had done for his followers by teaching them to pray. Then—a Prayer in response to prayer—the Paternoster, probably in a first shape, was spoken. Given to these special suppliants for their immediate use, it held not a word to identify it with any one time or race.

Using the Prayer

One who was no more than a devout Jew
of this age assuredly would have included
in it a prayer for the Jewish nation.
None could doubt the patriotism of
Jesus who listened to His words or saw
Him weep over Jerusalem. But, whatever the human limitations of knowledge
to which He submitted, we cannot doubt
His consciousness of speaking not merely
to those around Him but also to far-off
generations. This consciousness, this
deliberate aim to make His words such
as would keep their full meaning in time
to come, was a feature of His work that
all of us must have noticed. People
approach Him with some local question
of the day—about an inheritance, perhaps, or a detail of Sabbath-keeping, or
the payment of tribute. It had been
easy for Him to satisfy each of those who
came with a decision upon the special
problem of the moment. Such an
answer, however, would have lost the
most of its usefulness when the particular circumstances and habits which

gave rise to the question had passed away. Instead of this easier method, Jesus was ever at pains to reply by laying down a general principle of abiding validity, such as would guide His disciples in every age.

Nowhere, perhaps, is this Divine timelessness shown more strikingly than in the Lord's Prayer. Here He might have met the request made to him—as any merely human teacher had done—by setting forth a prayer entirely suitable to the special needs and special aspirations of first-century Palestinian Jews. Instead, He gave that which would serve the perennial needs of all mankind. Attempts have been made to find parallels between its petitions and phrases found in Jewish devotions of supposedly pre-Christian date. Some of these, in point of fact, seem only later to have been put into their existing form. But many of the resemblances are so slight as to be fanciful. And if every clause of the Paternoster could be matched by some stray sentence picked from the vast mass of Jewish

religious writings, the originality of the
Prayer itself would scarce seem lessened.
For this lies in its structure, its spirit,
its wonderful blending of brevity in form
with comprehensiveness in meaning. Because we are so familiar with it, we do not
always recognize its marvel. It suits the
twentieth century no less well than it
suited the first. There is not a word in
it to tie it down to any one land or time.
It is beloved alike by Christians who
differ on a score of important points. It
seems as much in place in some distant
mission station—where, probably, it is
the first written word to be translated—
as in St. Paul's in London, or in St.
Peter's at Rome. It can be lisped with
understanding by a young child. It
astonishes the wisest by its profundity.
Its larger—the Matthæan—form consists,
in Greek, of fifty-seven words. What is
there that we can desire to ask, what need
is there of human life, which these
astoundingly few sentences fail to express ? Yes, the more we ponder and

use these words, the surer we grow concerning Him Who spake them.

Therefore, knowing this Master to be
Divine, how comforting is their revelation
of the mind of God ! This Prayer shows
that He understands and feels with us
in our needs and difficulties. They have
no hint of anger to be appeased by reason
of our distrust, our failures, our weakness
in face of temptation. But there is
encouragement to tell God of these
things, and to ask His help. And the
fact that He bids us ask is itself a pledge
that the Prayer will be answered. There
are times when we grow impatient with
ourselves, and depressed by the frailty
of our characters. Then that word of
God which the Prayer enshrines bids
us turn to Him for pardon and strength,
and so go forward with braver hearts along
our road.

The better we know and use the Lord's
Prayer—the testimony of myriads confirms this belief—the greater will seem its
value. And so the more readily shall we

add to its petitions some words of thanks-giving. Not merely for those Divine mercies at large which richly bless our lives, but, in particular, for the gift of this Prayer shall we praise God—for its beauty, its teaching, its helpfulness, its encouragement. With such thoughts in our hearts, we shall follow the example of the Church in early days. Having said our Lord's Prayer as He taught it, with humble awe and overflowing thank-fulness we shall add :

" For Thine is the Kingdom,
The Power, and the Glory,
For ever and ever !   Amen."

THE END